HAMMOND PUBLIC LIBRARY

3 1161 00626 6780

P9-DMR-822

y583.75 GENT 1996
Gentle, Victor.
Venus fly traps and
 waterwheels

FEB 0 2 1998

HAMMOND PUBLIC LIBRARY
INDIANA
(219) 931-5100

	HPL	HPY	
EBH	HAN	HOW	HPK
LIN	RUP	SAW	CLC

THIS BOOK IS RENEWABLE BY PHONE OR IN
PERSON IF THERE IS NO RESERVE WAITING.

DEMCO

WITHDRAWN

BLOODTHIRSTY PLANTS

AN IMAGINATION LIBRARY SERIES

VENUS FLY TRAPS AND WATERWHEELS

Spring Traps of the Plant World

By Victor Gentle

With special thanks to the people at
the Carolina Biological Supply Company
and Peter Paul's Nursery,
and to Mr. Isao Takai,
for their kind encouragement and help.

Gareth Stevens Publishing
MILWAUKEE

HAMMOND PUBLIC LIBRARY
HAMMOND, IN

For a free color catalog describing Gareth Stevens' list of high-quality books and multimedia programs, call 1-800-542-2595 (USA) or 1-800-461-9120 (Canada). Gareth Stevens Publishing's Fax: (414) 225-0377. See our catalog, too, on the World Wide Web: http://gsinc.com

Library of Congress Cataloging-in-Publication Data

Gentle, Victor.
  Venus fly traps and waterwheels: spring traps of the plant world / by Victor Gentle.
    p. cm. — (Bloodthirsty plants)
  Includes bibliographical references (p. 23) and index.
  Summary: Describes the physical characteristics of these carnivorous plants and how they trap and digest their insect prey.
  ISBN 0-8368-1659-5 (lib. bdg.)
    1. Venus's flytrap–Juvenile literature. 2. Waterwheel plant–Juvenile literature. [1. Venus's flytrap. 2. Waterwheel plant. 3. Carnivorous plants.] I. Title. II. Series: Gentle, Victor. Bloodthirsty plants.
  QK495.D76G465   1996
  583'.121–dc20   96-12511

First published in 1996 by
Gareth Stevens Publishing
1555 North RiverCenter Drive, Suite 201
Milwaukee, WI 53212 USA

Text: Victor Gentle
Page layout: Victor Gentle and Karen Knutson
Cover design: Karen Knutson
Photo credits: Cover (main), p. 5 © 1993 David M. Dennis/Tom Stack & Associates; cover (background) © Stuart Wasserman/Picture Perfect; p. 7 © Kevin Adams; p. 9 © Visuals Unlimited/H. A. Miller 1978; p. 11 © Kerry T. Givens 1985/Tom Stack & Associates; p. 13 © Patricia Pietropaolo/Peter Paul's Nursery; pp. 15, 19 © Isao Takai; p. 17 © Visuals Unlimited/T. E. Adams; p. 21 © Visuals Unlimited/David Sieren

© 1996 by Gareth Stevens, Inc. All rights reserved to Gareth Stevens, Inc. No part of this book may be reproduced, stored in a retrieval system, or transmitted in any form or by any means, electronic, mechanical, photocopying, recording, or otherwise, without the prior written permission of the publisher except for the inclusion of brief acknowledged quotations in a review.

Printed in the United States of America

1 2 3 4 5 6 7 8 9 01 00 99 98 97 96

y583.75 GENT 1996
Gentle, Victor.
Venus fly traps and
 waterwheels

TABLE OF CONTENTS

SURPRISE!

It is a warm day in July, near the Cape Fear River in North Carolina. Small red and green plants are growing in a wet, swampy area. A sweet smell wafts from the spiky leaves on the plants.

Attracted by the sweet smell, a fly lands on one of the leaves. It crawls forward. Softly, it brushes two tiny hairs on the leaf's surface. Zap! The two parts of the leaf snap shut. The fly struggles briefly, but it is too late. There is no escape.

The trap of the Venus fly trap snaps shut in one-twentieth of a second. The **prey** (this time it's a fly) doesn't stand a chance.

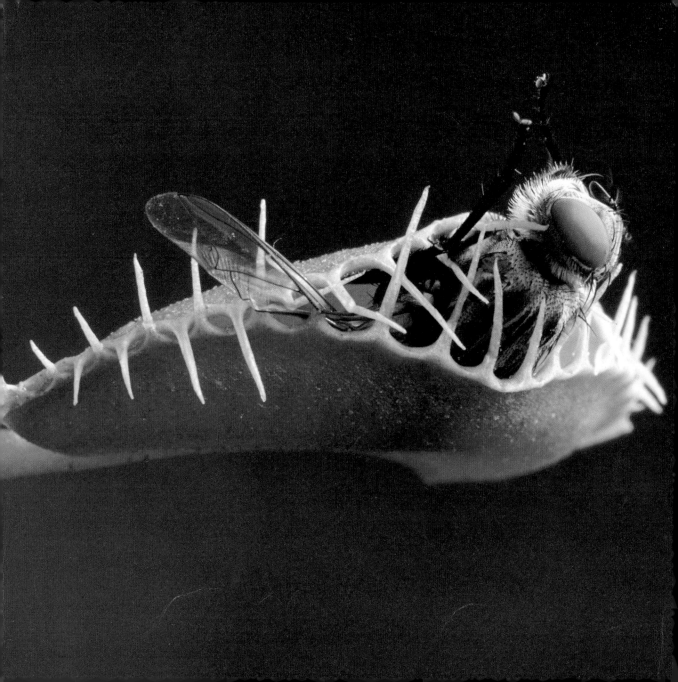

A TASTY MEAL FOR A VENUS FLY TRAP

The unhappy fly has been caught by a Venus fly trap. The Venus fly trap is probably the most famous of all **carnivorous** plants – that is, plants that eat animals!

Ants, flies, moths, beetles, grasshoppers – even worms – are no match for the grip of a Venus fly trap. Once caught, the tiny animal is slowly crushed by the jaws of the strong, claw-like leaf. The two halves of the leaf make a watertight container.

Then the Venus fly trap begins to **digest** its meal.

The trap of the Venus fly trap makes a tight seal around the insect it has just caught. The two sides of the trap actually grow shut to make the seal.

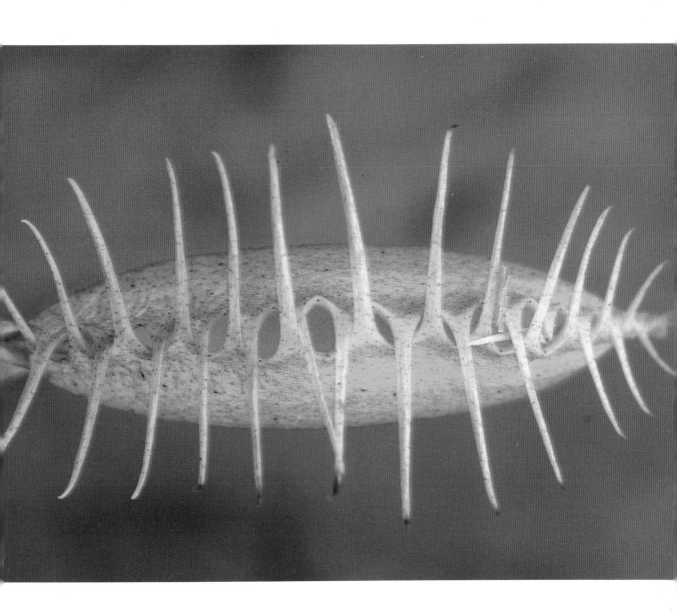

SPITTING OUT THE LEFTOVERS

As soon as the leafy trap is sealed tightly, **acids** and **enzymes** pour over the victim. These special liquids dissolve the good, nutritious parts of the insect. They leave behind the hard pieces – such as wings and bits of skeleton. Some days later, the leaves open up again, and the leftovers fall out. The Venus fly trap is ready for action again.

Here, the remains of a grasshopper are visible. After a while, they will dry out and drop to the ground.

WHERE DO VENUS FLY TRAPS GROW?

The scientific name for the Venus fly trap is *Dionaea muscipula* (die-uh-NEE-yuh muh-SKIP-yoo-luh). It grows wild naturally in only one small part of the world — a few swampy areas in North and South Carolina in the United States. But it's not hard to grow at home. Amateur **botanists** in many parts of the world grow them. In the wild, however, the Venus fly trap is an endangered **species**.

A Venus fly trap has caught a tasty meal – it's another grasshopper. This plant is about 6 or 7 inches (15 to 18 centimeters) tall.

MEET THE WATERWHEEL PLANT

Only one other kind of plant uses spring traps — the waterwheel plant.

Waterwheel plants look a little like light green, hairy, wet caterpillars! They grow to between 6 and 10 inches (15 and 25 cm) long.

Unlike Venus fly traps, waterwheel plants have no roots. They do not live on land. Instead, they float just under the water's surface near reeds and rushes. Swamps and lakes are their home.

A waterwheel plant, or *Aldrovanda vesiculosa* (al-droe-VAN-duh vuh-SIK-yoo-LOE-suh), with rings of eight traps. In this photo, it is about 5 times bigger than life size.

A HUNDRED TRAPS — AND MORE!

Like Venus fly traps, waterwheel plants are also carnivorous. They like to eat small **aquatic** creatures – animals that live in the water.

Each waterwheel plant can have more than one hundred traps. The traps are arranged in eights, like spokes of a wheel. Each trap has four to eight long bristles for little animals to cling on to. Each trap also has about forty small trigger hairs. When a small animal touches the tiny trigger hairs, the trap snaps shut.

Rootless waterwheel plants can have up to one hundred traps – or more. These waterwheel plants are from Japan.

WHAT WATERWHEEL PLANTS EAT

Waterwheel plants prey on *Daphnia* (DAFF-nee-uh), which are water fleas, and other tiny animals that live in the water. Each trap snaps shut in one-fiftieth of a second. It takes a few days for a trap to digest a good-sized meal. Then the trap is open for business again. But if a trap catches a small animal that is too big for it, it will never reopen. Instead, the trap will wither and die.

A species of water flea, *Ceriodaphnia pulex* (SEER-ee-oh-DAFF-nyuh POO-lex), is shown here about 300 times life size.

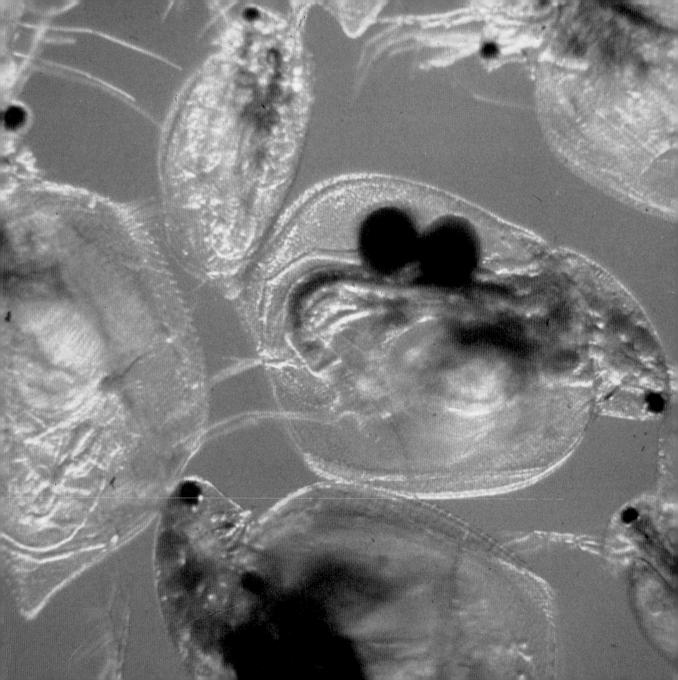

WHERE WATERWHEEL PLANTS LIVE

Unlike the Venus fly trap, waterwheel plants are found in many places in the world. They live in parts of Europe, Africa, India, Japan, and Australia. They are not found in the wild anywhere in North or South America.

The scientific name for the **genus** of waterwheel plants is *Aldrovanda*. There is only one species of waterwheel plant, which is divided into four very similar **subspecies**. The subspecies from India is the largest – up to 10 inches (25 cm) long.

The Japanese subspecies of the waterwheel plant, with its beautiful, tiny, white flower, rising above the surface of the water.

IT'S A JUNGLE OUT THERE!

The spring trap is not the only way for a plant to catch insects and other small animals.

The sundews trap insects and small animals with a sweet, sticky liquid. Once caught, victims cannot struggle free. Others, the bladderworts, have traps that suck in their tiny prey like a vacuum cleaner. Pitcher plants drown their victims in a colorful jug full of digestive juices. (Some pitcher plants can **absorb** animals as big as small frogs and mice.) Some carnivorous **fungi** even lasso their prey!

You can learn more about the strange and wonderful world of carnivorous plants by reading other books. You can also learn more about them by growing some yourself and watching closely.

A Venus fly trap, from above, growing wild in North Carolina next to another carnivorous plant, a sundew, *Drosera brevifolia* (DROSS-er-uh bre-vi-FOE-lyuh).

GROW YOUR OWN VENUS FLY TRAPS

Venus fly traps are fairly easy to grow. Like most other carnivorous plants, they need **humid** conditions and plenty of water. Rainwater is better than tap water. Keeping a partially open cover on your growing container will help keep the humidity level high.

The best soil is sphagnum moss. Nearby garden centers should have this. And you can experiment with other light, airy, moisture-holding soils.

A garden center, or a science supply company that supplies Venus fly trap bulbs, will usually give detailed instructions. Try it!

WHERE TO GET PLANTS OR SEEDS

Here are some addresses of carnivorous plant suppliers. For other sources, contact a club or society listed on the next page.

Carolina Biological Supply
   Company
2700 York Road
Burlington, NC 27215 USA

Exotica Plants
Community Mail Bag
Cordalba
QLD 4660 Australia

Peter Paul's Nursery
4665 Chapin Road
Canandaigua, NY 14424
USA

MORE TO READ AND VIEW

Books (nonfiction): *Bladderworts: Trapdoors to Oblivion.* Victor Gentle (Gareth Stevens)
Butterworts: Greasy Cups of Death. Victor Gentle (Gareth Stevens)
Carnivorous Mushrooms: Lassoing Their Prey? Victor Gentle (Gareth Stevens)
Carnivorous Plants. Nancy J. Nielsen (Franklin Watts)
Killer Plants. Mycol Doyle (Lowell House Juvenile)
Pitcher Plants: The Elegant Insect Traps. Carol Lerner (Morrow)
Pitcher Plants: Slippery Pits of No Escape. Victor Gentle (Gareth Stevens)
Plants of Prey. Densey Clyne (Gareth Stevens)
Sundews: A Sweet and Sticky Death. Victor Gentle (Gareth Stevens)

Books (fiction): *Elizabite: Adventures of a Carnivorous Plant.* H.A. Rey (Linnet)
Island of Doom. Richard Brightfield (Gareth Stevens)

Videos (nonfiction): *Carnivorous Plants.* (Oxford Scientific Films)

Videos (fiction): *The Day of the Triffids* and *The Little Shop of Horrors* are fun to watch.

WHERE TO WRITE TO FIND OUT MORE

Your community may have a local chapter of a carnivorous plant society. Try looking it up in the telephone directory. Or contact one of the following national organizations:

Australia
Australian Carnivorous Plant Society, Inc.
P.O. Box 391
St. Agnes, South Australia 5097 Australia

New Zealand
New Zealand Carnivorous Plant Society
P.O. Box 21-381, Henderson
Auckland, New Zealand

United Kingdom
The Carnivorous Plant Society
174 Baldwins Lane, Croxley Green
Hertfordshire WD3 3LQ
England

Canada
Eastern Carnivorous Plant Society
Dionaea, 23 Cherryhill Drive
Grimsby, Ontario, Canada L3M 3B3

South Africa – has no CP society, but
a supplier to contact is:
Eric Green, 11 Wepener Street
Southfield, 7800, Cape, South Africa

United States
International Carnivorous Plant Society
Fullerton Arboretum
California State University at Fullerton
Fullerton, CA 92634 USA

If you are on the Internet, or otherwise on-line, you can call up a World Wide Web page that gives links to other Web pages of interest to carnivorous plant enthusiasts: http://www.cvp.com/feedme/links.html

GLOSSARY

You can find these words on the pages listed. Reading a word in a sentence helps you understand it even better.

absorb (uhb-ZORB) — to soak up inside 20

acids (ASS-ids) — harsh liquids that can dissolve many things 8

aquatic (uh-KWAH-tic) — living or growing in water 14

botanists (BOT-uh-nists) — scientists who study plants 10

carnivorous (kar-NIV-er-us) — flesh-eating 6, 14, 20, 22

digest (die-JEST) — to break into bits that the body can use for food 6, 16

enzymes (EN-zimes) — special substances that help digestion 8

fungi (FUN-JYE) — the plural of **fungus** — a type of plant whose main feature is that it has none of the special green substance found in most leafy plants, so it can't make its own food from sunlight, air, and water 20

genus (JEE-nus) — plural: **genera** — a group of closely related plants or animals, although sometimes a plant or animal may be so unlike any other, there may be only one member, or species, in the group 18

humid (HYOO-mid) — damp 22

prey (PRAY) — a victim of a hunter, trapper, or trap 4, 16, 20

species (SPEE-shees) — an individual type of plant or animal; closely related plants or animals within a genus 10, 16, 18

subspecies — a plant or animal that is so similar to another that botanists don't want to call it a separate species 18

INDEX

24

3 1161 00626 6780